To . . . .

From . . . .

the delinquent fairy's thoughts on
dieting

lauren white

 SOURCEBOOKS, INC.
NAPERVILLE, ILLINOIS

INTRODUCTION

Hi my name is Flo — the
Fairy with aTTitude!
I have BEEN descRibeD,
(I Think raTher unkinDly)
as DElinQUEnT —

I personally prefer the term "Alternative"...

I understand the pressures modern life places on today's Woman/Fairy: Juggling Kids, Careers, and Cream Cakes...

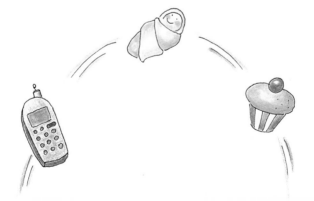

Anyhow, wHen it comeS to waTcHing mY Weight — I've been There, done THat, got the T-shiRt...

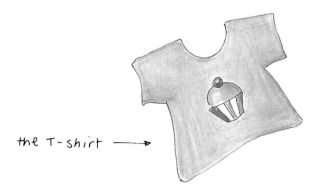

the T-shirt ⟶

So, I Thought I'd share SomE

of My experience With you in This little book of Useful hints and Tips

Remember: You WiLL need:

* WiLLpower
* Strength of Character
* To know how To chEat

(chocolate chip ice cream stain) →

CALORIES - A GUIDE

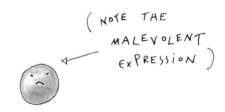

(NOTE THE MALEVOLENT EXPRESSION)

introducing the calorie

and here are some of his friends

hic!

the red wine calorie

the comfort food calorie

the T.V dinner calorie

Z z z

the midnight snack calorie

the fast food calorie

m m m

the chocolate calorie

CALORIE COMBAT STRATEGY Nº 1

use a fork........

(small pile
of calories)

......the calories will fall through the tines........

DIET DEFINITIONS

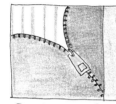

THINGS THAT DON'T DO UP WHEN YOU WANT THEM TO.....

ZIPS

IN URGENT NEED OF CREAM CAKES !!

SUPER MODELS

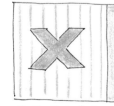

"I DON'T KNOW WHAT YOU MEAN"...

DENIAL

LYING TO AD!

MIRROR

A SQUARE MEAL
— IF YOU'RE A RABBIT

CARROT

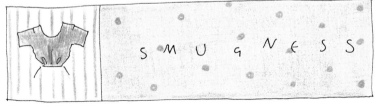

SMUGNESS

T — SHIRT
(tucked in...)

COLOR

YOU CAN ROUGHLY GUESS THE CALORIE CONTENT OF A FOOD BY ITS COLOR ...

e.g.

peas

melon

orange sorbet

GREEN → very safe ..... YELLOW → still quite safe .... ORANGE → caution ....

jelly

double chocolate chip
fudge cake !

just
don't
eat
anything
blue ...

| RED | BROWN | BLUE |

.... danger zone .... aah !!!! ..... no problem !

CALORIES - A GUIDE

there's never just one...

..they go around in gangs...

DON'T

wear horizontal stripes!

REDUCE YOUR SIZE IN LESS THAN 5 MINUTES !!!

· YOU WILL NEED ·

scissors

needle

thread

oh..... and a thin friend.....

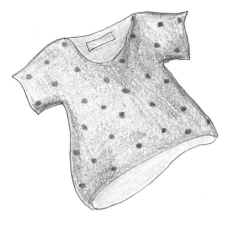

carefully
cut out
the size
labels
from your
thin friend's
clothes and
sew into
your own
clothes.

SIZE:
Tiny

VOiLA!

CALORIES - A GUIDE

they hang around in bars...

THE
WISDOM
OF
FLO

...cookies are good for you.......

REFRIGERATOR

PLEASURE PALACE!

NO... NO... NO... NO.... YES...

WILL POWER

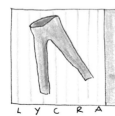

HEAVEN SENT

LYCRA

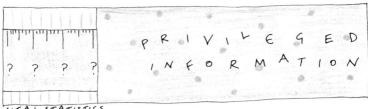

VITAL STATISTICS

CELLULITE

TEMPTATION

CALORIE COMBAT
STRATEGY Nº 2

barbecue your food . . . . . .

...and the calories burn away......

ping!

CALORIES - A GUIDE

it's global warfare!...

the international lineup. . . .

the chop suey calorie

"la baguette" calorie

the turkish delight calorie

the curry calorie

the fish and chips calorie

the beef steak calorie

D o

check your weight...

THE
WISDOM
OF
FLO

.... size DOES matter..........

SOUND

LISTEN TO YOUR FOOD TO ESTIMATE ITS CALORIES...

e.g

crispbread	apple	banana
CRISPY	CRUNCHY	SQUASHY

very good .... O.K. .... beware ....

CALORIE COMBAT
STRATEGY Nº 3

 break a cookie......

....and half the calories drop out!......

CALORIES - A GUIDE

they come in all shapes and sizes...

these are just a few little pests...

the noodle calorie

the avocado calorie

the burger calorie

the cheese calorie

the raisin calorie

the banana calorie

How to Weigh Yourself

STEP ONE —

Make a note of your clothes...

(weight of clothes

TO BE DEDUCTED LATER...)

woolly socks

scarf

bobble hat

mittens

bag — and contents !!!

STEP TWO —

climb onto the scales.............

STEP THREE...

think positive.

STEP FOUR

take gravity into account.....

$E = Mc_2 \div 4$

$3(2 \times 53) = \dfrac{14}{6}$

$34\overline{)241}$

$14 \times 6 \times 2 \div \times (AB)$

$= 68000_2 +$

$= 16^3$

42

STEP FIVE...

calculate accurate weight...

me... minus heavy clothes...

plus positive thoughts...

minus effects of gravity...

... or just think of a

number .... and

halve it !

CALORIE COMBAT
STRATEGY № 4

eat outdoors......

...and the calories blow away........

D o

put a lock on the refrigerator...

D O N ' T

...throw away the key !...

CALORIES – A GUIDE

seduction is second nature...

. boredom .

. bliss .

THE
WISDOM
OF
FLO

..... clothes SHRINK in

storage......

(last summer's T-shirt)

CALORIE COMBAT
STRATEGY Nº 5

alcoholic calories.......

(unused
calories
hic!)

..... sink to the bottom of the glass!.....

CALORIES - A GUIDE

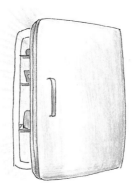

the natural habitat!

THE FLO PLAN DIET....
day 1

breakfast	GLASS WATER	(1)
mid-morning	APPLE	(1)
lunch	GRAPES	(5)
afternoon	GLASS WATER	(2)
dinner	BAKED POTATO (NO BUTTER)	(1)
result:	PAIN	

(or tell it how it is) →

day 2

SLICE TOAST	(1½)
APPLE	(2)
LETTUCE LEAF	(3)
GLASS JUICE	(1)
CHICKEN BREAST (GRILLED — SKINLESS)	(1)
BOREDOM	

THE FLO PLAN DIET — CONT'D

day 3

breakfast	(LARGE) BOWL MUESLI + SLICE TOAST	(1)
mid-morning	COOKIE	(1)
lunch	LETTUCE LEAVES (WITH DRESSING)	(14)
afternoon	(SMALL) PIECE CHOCOLATE	(2)
dinner	CHICKEN LEG (FRIED WITH CRISPY SKIN!...)	(1)
result:	OUCH!	

day 4

PANCAKE
(+ MAPLE SYRUP)

COFFEE (+ CREAM)

FRENCH FRIES
(PIPING HOT, SMOTHERED IN KETCHUP!)

DOUGHNUTS

PIZZA
GARLIC BREAD
CHEESECAKE (+ CREAM)
RED WINE

WELCOME HOME!

CALORIES - A GUIDE

they're not all bad guys...

goody two- shoes calories :

the lettuce calorie

the rice calorie

the tomato calorie

the granary bread calorie

the lemon calorie

the apple calorie

DON'T

... be ridiculous!...

THE WISDOM OF FLO

...carrots are

GOOD for you....

......chocolate   is BETTER ! ......

CALORIE COMBAT

STRATEGY Nº 6

microwave your food........

(Flo "microwaving"!!!)

...... and deactivate the calories !......

keep well-stocked cupboards...

...shop when you're hungry!

CALORIES - A GUIDE

calories love holidays...

and here are some fun-loving types...

the halloween calorie

the cruise calorie

the birthday calorie

the weekend calorie

the in-flight calorie

the Christmas calorie

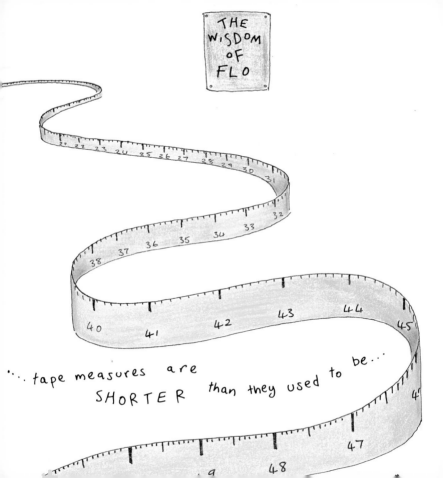

CALORIE COMBAT
STRATEGY Nº 7

eat out·······

.....the calories belong to the person who pays!......

THE BILL

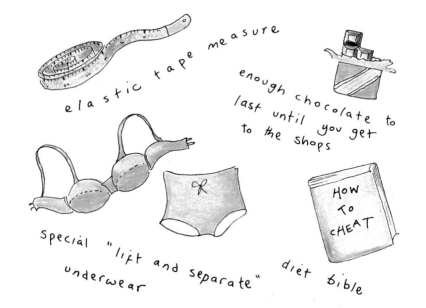

EMERGENCY KIT

elastic tape measure

enough chocolate to last until you get to the shops

special "lift and separate" underwear

diet bible

HOW TO CHEAT

ankle-slimming heels

small mirror to check for "chocolate mustache"

last resort trick T-shirt!

CALORIES - A GUIDE

double chocolate chip ice cream — with extra chocolate...

...the biggest villain of them all...

CALORIE COMBAT
STRATEGY Nº 8

e a t   i c e   c r e a m · · · · · ·

inert
calories

......freezing neutralizes calories!.....

REMEMBER

LIFE'S
TOO SHORT
TO COUNT

EVERY CALORIE.....

Lauren White spent much of her childhood at the bottom of the garden involved in a fruitless search for a real live fairy! Many years later, up popped Flo: Lauren comments "You imagine a shy, delicate creature with shimmering wings and a bell-like laugh—I got saddled with Flo!"

Flo has an opinion on everything. She's mischievous, subversive, and likes taking a very wry look at the antics of mortals. Lauren has managed to capture some of Flo's thoughts on aspects of the human condition and set them down in this little book.

Flo and Lauren live in the village of Cranfield in Bedfordshire, England, with Michael (mortal) and Jack (canine; terrified of Flo), where Lauren spends her spare time sketching, playing the piano, and adding to her collection of Victorian pixie lights (53 at present) by scouring antique shops and fairs. She has produced gift books celebrating life, books of spells (with Flo's guidance), and her designs for Hotchpotch greetings cards are sold around the world.

Sourcebooks, Inc.
P.O. Box 4410, Naperville, Illinois 60567-4410

(630) 961-3900
FAX: (630) 961-2168

Printed and bound in Spain

MQ 10 9 8 7 6 5 4 3 2 1

ISBN: 1-57071-639-0